973
POR

n

Massachuets

c 2

Copyright © 1996 Steck-Vaughn Company

Steck-Vaughn Company

Executive Editor	Diane Sharpe
Senior Editor	Martin S. Saiewitz
Design Manager	Pamela Heaney
Photo Editor	Margie Foster

Proof Positive/Farrowlyne Associates, Inc.
Program Editorial, Revision Development, Design, and Production

Consultant: Tara G. Frier, Director of Communications, Executive Office of Communities and Development

Published by Raintree Steck-Vaughn Publishers, an imprint of Steck-Vaughn Company.

A Turner Educational Services, Inc. book. Based on the Portrait of America television series by R. E. (Ted) Turner.

Cover Photo: Autumn color by © Michael Reagan.

Library of Congress Cataloging-in-Publication Data

Thompson, Kathleen.
    Massachusetts / Kathleen Thompson.
      p.   cm. — (Portrait of America)
    "A Turner book."
    "Based on the Portrait of America television series"—T.p. verso.
    Includes index.
    ISBN 0-8114-7341-4 (library binding).—ISBN 0-8114-7446-1 (softcover)
    1. Massachusetts—Juvenile literature. [1. Massachusetts].
I. Title. II. Series: Thompson, Kathleen. Portrait of America.
F64.3.T48 1996
974.4—dc20   95-45250
                                       CIP
                                       AC

Printed and Bound in the United States of America

4 5 6 7 8 9 10 WZ 03 02 01 00

Acknowledgments
The publishers wish to thank the following for permission to reproduce photographs:
P. 7 © Henryk Kaiser/Southern Stock; p. 8 Plimoth Plantation, Inc.; p. 11 courtesy of Plymouth County Development Council; p. 12 (top) Massachusetts Historical Society, (bottom) Peabody Essex Museum, Salem, Massachusetts, photo by Mark Sexton; p. 13 Massachusetts Historical Society; p. 14 Boston Convention and Visitors Bureau; p. 15 North Wind Picture Archive; p. 16 The Bettmann Archive; p. 17 North Wind Picture Archive; p. 18 U.S. Navy; p. 19 © Michael Reagan; p. 20 U.S. Senate; p. 21 John F. Kennedy Library; p. 22 The Museum of Fine Arts, Boston; p. 23 (top) North Wind Picture Archive, (bottom) The Old North Church; p. 24 North Wind Picture Archive; p. 25 © Michael Reagan; pp. 26, 27 (both) Cape Cod Chamber of Commerce; p. 28 © Donna Coveney/MIT Photo; pp. 30, 31 (both) Cape Cod Chamber of Commerce; p. 32 Lowell Museum; p. 33 Lowell Historical Society; p. 34 © Michael Reagan; p. 36 (top, middle left) © Michael Reagan, (middle right) Concord Museum; p. 37 (top) The Bettmann Archive, (bottom) Longfellow National Historic Site/National Park Service; p. 38 (top) UPI/Bettmann, (bottom) Collection of Mr. and Mrs. Paul Mellon, Upperville, Virginia; p. 39 John Fitzgerald Kennedy National Historic Site/National Park Service; pp. 40, 41 (both) National Center for Afro-American Artists; p. 42 © Michael Reagan; p. 44 Photo Courtesy of Kevin A. Kirwin/RVA/MWRA; p. 46 One Mile Up; p. 47 (left) One Mile Up, (middle) © RC W. Greene/Vireo, (right) © Jack Wilburn/Earth Scenes.

STECK-VAUGHN

PORTRAIT OF AMERICA

Massachusetts

Kathleen Thompson

A Turner Book

RSVP

RAINTREE
STECK-VAUGHN
PUBLISHERS
The Steck-Vaughn Company

Austin, Texas

Massachusetts

Haverhill

Lawrence
Lowell
Fitchburg

Merrimack River

Rockport
Gloucester

Mount
Greylock ▲

Salem

Leominster

MINUTE MAN NATIONAL
HISTORIC PARK ■

Cambridge

Connecticut River

Pittsfield

Quabbin
Reservoir

Waltham

Framingham

☆ BOSTON

Amherst   Worcester

Northhampton

Holyoke

Provincetown

BERKSHIRE
HILLS

Brockton

Springfield

Plymouth

CAPE COD

Taunton

Fall River   New Bedford

MARTHA'S VINEYARD

NANTUCKET
ISLAND

Contents

Introduction

Massachusetts has been the site of so much United States history, you could think of it as a grandparent state. The Pilgrims landing at Plymouth, the battles at Lexington and Concord, and the Boston Tea Party are well-known to us from the early episodes in the story of our country. They all happened in Massachusetts. Now the state is as much a model for the future as a reminder of the past. Over the years the people of Massachusetts have made their state a leader in education and in the arts. It was one of the first states to enact laws protecting wetlands and many forms of wildlife. Today Massachusetts leads the East Coast in high technology. Its future is as glowing as its past.

Boston is one of the oldest cities in the United States. Historic landmarks are carefully preserved among modern skyscrapers.

Massachusetts

Cape Cod, the Berkshires, Atlantic seaport

*I*n the Forefront of History

Before European explorers began arriving in the early 1500s, present-day Massachusetts was the home of several Native American groups. Among them were Massachusett, Mohican, Nauset, Nipmuc, Pennacook, Pocomtuc, and Wampanoag. Except for the Mohican, all of these were members of the powerful Algonquian nation. These groups lived in permanent villages. They hunted, fished, and grew maize (corn), beans, and pumpkins.

At one time at least thirty thousand Native Americans lived in the Massachusetts area. But the European explorers who came into contact with these groups passed on infectious and deadly diseases. The Native Americans had no defenses against these diseases, and they died by the thousands. By the time the Pilgrims landed at Plymouth, more than a century later, there were only about seven thousand Native Americans left in the area.

The first known Europeans to visit the area were a group led by Portuguese sailor Miguel Cortereal. They

The *Mayflower II* is a modern reproduction of how the original ship is thought to have looked. In 1970 this ship was sailed across the Atlantic to celebrate the 350th anniversary of the Pilgrims' voyage.

were shipwrecked off the coast of present-day Massachusetts in 1502. Cortereal and his crew lived with the local Native Americans for at least nine years, and Cortereal was made a chief. In 1602 Bartholomew Gosnold, an English explorer, built a house and a fort on Cape Cod, a peninsula off the coast of Massachusetts. He liked the place so much that he planned to establish a permanent settlement. But a supply shortage made him abandon his plan.

Captain John Smith of Virginia arrived in Massachusetts in 1614. He gave the name *New England* to the areas that are now Massachusetts, Maine, Connecticut, New Hampshire, Vermont, and Rhode Island. He made a map of New England on which the word *Massachusetts* was used for the first time. He named the place after one group of Native Americans that lived there. Smith also wrote a book about New England. In it he called Massachusetts "the paradise of all those parts," and said, "I would rather live here than anywhere."

This description of New England was read by a small group of English people living in Holland. At that time the Church of England was the official religion of the country. This group had argued with the Church of England and wanted to start their own church. They were called Separatists because they wanted to separate from the Church of England. That was illegal in England, so in 1608 they had fled to Holland to avoid being sent to jail. By 1616, when Smith's book was published, many of the Separatists were tired of living in Holland. They wanted to live in a country where English was spoken and where they wouldn't be looked upon as foreigners. They wanted a place where they could practice their religion without fear of persecution. Massachusetts sounded like the ideal place.

The Separatists boarded a small ship, the *Speedwell*, which carried them from Holland to Southampton, England. There they joined another group of Separatists. After some delays the voyagers regrouped at Plymouth, England. On September 16, 1620, 102 passengers sailed from Plymouth aboard the *Mayflower*. The 180-ton *Mayflower* was only ninety feet long and badly overloaded. The travelers called themselves Pilgrims, which is a word that describes people on a holy journey. The voyage across the stormy Atlantic Ocean took more than two months. Finally on November 19, 1620, the Pilgrims sighted Cape Cod.

Plymouth Rock is the landmark where the Pilgrims stepped ashore in 1620 to found the first permanent colony in New England.

During the next month, members of the expedition explored the coast of Cape Cod. The Pilgrims established a permanent settlement at a place they called Plymouth.

Because it was wintertime when they landed, there was no time to plant and harvest crops. The Pilgrims did not have enough supplies to feed themselves until a crop could be grown. Half of them died that first

John Winthrop was the leader of the Puritan colonists. He founded a settlement near present-day Boston.

winter. The survivors were greatly helped by a Native American known as Squanto who could speak English. Squanto served as an interpreter and introduced the Pilgrims to Massasoit, the chief of the Wampanoag. The Wampanoag taught the Pilgrims about new foods and ways to hunt, fish, plant, and cook in the new land. By the next fall, the colony was self-sufficient. The colonists celebrated the first Thanksgiving and invited about ninety Wampanoag. They shared turkey and pumpkin as well as venison, eels, clams, and wild plums.

In 1628 another religious group established the Massachusetts Bay Colony, about fifty miles north of Plymouth. This group also came because they disagreed with the Church of England. But they did not want to separate from the church. Instead they wanted to reform it. They were called Puritans because they

Nineteen men and women in Salem were hanged for witchcraft in 1692. This 1855 painting by T. H. Matteson depicts the witchcraft trial of George Jacobs.

wanted to practice a "purified" form of that religion. The Puritans lived by strict rules that dictated every detail of a person's life. These rules were enforced by Governor John Winthrop. In 1630 more than a thousand Puritans in 11 ships sailed from England to America. Some settled in Boston, and others founded a colony in Salem.

Boston soon became an educational and cultural center. Before the end of the century, Boston established the first public park in the country, the first public school, the first college, the first post office, and the first newspaper.

The early friendship between Native Americans and colonists grew cold as more and more colonies were set up on land taken over from Native Americans. Metacomet, a Native American leader whom the colonists called "King Philip," led an uprising against the colonies. He was the son of Massasoit, who had first welcomed the settlers. Metacomet decided too many settlers had taken over his land, and he was determined to drive them away. Between 1675 and 1678, hundreds of Native Americans and colonists were killed in the fighting. In the end, the colonists, with their guns and larger numbers, defeated Metacomet's forces.

Meanwhile the colonies were also having trouble with Great Britain. The colonists were businesspeople. They built ships and traded goods with countries

Paul Revere made this engraving of how he imagined Metacomet, or "King Philip," might have looked.

Boston's Faneuil Hall Marketplace was built in the 1970s next to historic Faneuil Hall. In the late 1700s, Faneuil Hall served as a meeting place for colonists to discuss their grievances against the British.

around the world. But the British wanted the colonists to trade only with them. From about 1651 to 1733, the British passed a number of laws called the Navigation Acts. These laws stated that all goods for overseas trade had to be carried on ships owned by the British. Also, three quarters of the ships' crews had to be British. There were other laws, too. The colonists ignored most of them.

Massachusetts merchants were making a lot of money in overseas trade. They shipped dried fish, corn, salt, and lumber to the West Indies. They brought back cotton, dyes, tobacco, and molasses. They also shipped rum made from the molasses to Great Britain. These merchants were not about to stop such profitable trade. All the respectable merchants of Massachusetts became smugglers in the eyes of the British.

Then the British imposed the Stamp Act of 1765. The Stamp Act was the first direct tax imposed by Britain on its American colonies. The act placed a tax on certain documents and printed materials such as contracts, newspapers, and pamphlets. These materials had to carry a special stamp. The tax money was to pay for the cost of maintaining troops in the colonies. A group of colonists who opposed the Stamp Act formed a political group called the Sons of Liberty. The Sons of Liberty and other colonists opposed the Stamp Act not only because they did not want to pay the tax, but also because they had no representatives in the British Parliament. Therefore they had no vote on the taxes they had to pay. They rallied around the slogan, "No taxation without representation."

By 1770 the British had stationed four thousand soldiers in Boston. Some earned extra money doing local work during their off-duty hours. This meant they were taking away jobs from native Bostonians. On March 5, 1770, a mob of angry citizens gathered outside a building that soldiers were guarding. The mob called the soldiers names and then started to throw rocks and snowballs. The troops fired on the mob and hit Crispus Attucks, a former slave. Attucks and four other Bostonians were killed. Samuel Adams, one of the most radical patriots, called the event the "Boston Massacre."

Many Bostonians wanted revenge. However, some thought the soldiers deserved a fair trial. Samuel Adams' cousin, John Adams, had the courage to defend the soldiers. The court ruled that most of the soldiers had acted in self-defense. John Adams felt that the right to a fair trial should be a guiding principle for a free country. He later became the second President of the United States. His son John Quincy Adams became the sixth President.

Samuel Adams contributed greatly toward colonial freedom. He led the Boston Tea Party, served in the Second Continental Congress, and signed the Declaration of Independence.

In 1773 members of the Sons of Liberty dressed themselves as Native Americans and dumped a load of British tea into Boston Harbor to protest a tax on tea. News of the events that were occurring in Boston and elsewhere was communicated to other colonies by groups called committees of correspondence. All over the colonies, people began stockpiling guns and ammunition in case the British used force.

The British sent more soldiers to the colonies. Then, in April 1775, British soldiers were spotted heading toward Lexington and Concord, two towns northwest of Boston, where weapons were stored. Paul Revere rode on horseback to each of the towns to warn the citizens. When the British troops arrived first at Lexington and then at Concord, armed citizens were

The Boston Tea Party was one of the colonists' first open acts of rebellion against British laws and taxes.

waiting. Gunfire broke out. When the day was over, about one hundred of almost fifteen hundred colonists had been killed, wounded, or were missing. The British had over two hundred men killed, wounded, or missing. The Revolutionary War had begun.

One of the most famous battles of the war was Boston's Battle of Bunker Hill in June 1775. The British lost about one thousand men in the attack, and the victory helped boost the confidence of the colonial soldiers. Many battles were fought throughout the 13 colonies during the Revolutionary War. Finally, in 1783 the British and the Americans signed a treaty of peace, which guaranteed independence for the United States.

In 1788 Massachusetts approved the Constitution of the United States and became the sixth state. In its early years, Massachusetts continued to build ships and do business as traders. When France and Great Britain went to war in the early 1800s, shipping companies in Massachusetts saw a way to increase their trade business. They supplied European countries with the goods

This painting depicts the battle at Concord Bridge, which took place on April 10, 1775.

17

The U.S.S. *Constitution* was launched in Boston in 1797. The ship was involved in many sea battles, including those against the Barbary States and during the War of 1812. The ship remains in Boston Harbor as a monument to this country's freedom.

that were no longer coming from those two warring countries. However, the British and the French began interfering with the neutral American ships. In 1807 President Thomas Jefferson signed the Embargo Act, which was intended to punish Great Britain and France. This act prohibited American traders from doing business with either country. The plan only served to economically ruin American shipping companies, however. In 1812 the United States declared war with Great Britain. Shipping companies in Massachusetts opposed the war because they feared that their relationship with Great Britain and France would end. The War of 1812 finally ended when the British retreated into Canada in 1814. The United States had received very little help from Massachusetts.

The first half of the 1800s was prosperous for Massachusetts. Farming spread into the farthest valleys of the Berkshires. Toll roads, canals, and railroads were built connecting all of the principal cities. Factories were built along the rivers. The village of Lowell became a major cotton-textile manufacturing center because of the waterpower provided by the Merrimack River's Pawtucket Falls. The textile industry, which was to lead the state's economy for the next century, gained importance.

There was strong opposition in Massachusetts to slavery. In 1832 Bostonians formed the New England Anti-Slavery Society. When the Civil War broke out in 1861, the state sent about 150,000 men into service for the Union. Massachusetts was a major arsenal for the war, supplying goods such as guns, blankets, and tents.

During and after the war, thousands of immigrants poured into the cities of Massachusetts looking for work. Many of these immigrants were Irish who had fled their country to escape a famine. Many residents discriminated against the Irish because they did not want them competing for jobs. But the Irish moved into Massachusetts politics, and with political power, they were eventually able to shed the prejudice against them.

Other ethnic groups who came into Massachusetts followed the Irish example. And there were many of them. By 1900 about thirty percent of the population of Massachusetts had been born in another country. By 1920 about 67 percent were either foreign-born or had immigrant parents.

Manufacturing, which had been very profitable for Massachusetts, was marked by troubles in the early part of the twentieth century. Factory workers wanted to form unions to protect their rights. Owners, however, opposed anything that would weaken their control of their businesses. Also, many textile companies moved to new headquarters in southern states, where labor was cheaper. Health codes and building codes forced others to shut down.

Mount Holyoke College in South Hadley, founded in 1837, was the first women's college in the United States.

Service industries, however, began to assume a new role in the Massachusetts economy. Banking and insurance reached out for new markets in the West. Retail and wholesale trade expanded to serve the new urban populations. Many office and clerical jobs were created in cities such as Boston, Worcester, and Springfield.

When the Great Depression of the 1930s fell upon the United States, many people across the country became unemployed. Banks closed and the country's economy was brought to a standstill. Massachusetts was one of the few states that offered its people unemployment relief. When President Franklin D. Roosevelt was elected in 1932, his New Deal program brought similar relief to all the states. When the United States entered World War II in 1941, Massachusetts became a leading producer of war materials. The traditional industries of shipbuilding and machinery were greatly expanded, along with the development of new products such as radar, sonar, and jet engines.

The nation began to face its racial problems in the 1950s and 1960s. Massachusetts was no exception. Legislation was passed to prevent segregation in housing. In 1966 Edward Brooke of Massachusetts became the first African American to win a seat in the United States Senate in almost one hundred years.

Senator John F. Kennedy of Massachusetts became President of the United States in 1961. He served almost three years before he was assassinated. His

Edward Brooke was the first African American United States senator since Reconstruction.

This photo shows three of the Kennedy brothers in 1946. From left to right, they are John, Robert, and Edward.

brother Robert Kennedy served as attorney general during his term. Robert Kennedy was assassinated in 1968 while campaigning for the Democratic nomination for President. Their brother Edward M. Kennedy served as a United States senator from Massachusetts beginning in 1962.

Today Massachusetts has one of the most important areas of high-tech industry in the eastern United States. But substantial job losses in the manufacturing industry have caused economic problems. The state had lost so much money during the late 1980s that it was forced to increase income taxes in 1990. In spite of these economic difficulties, Massachusetts is working hard to maintain progress as it enters a new century.

Paul Revere's Role

Paul Revere was born in Boston in 1735. His father was a silversmith and taught his craft to his son. Revere was one of the finest silversmiths of his time, but he also experimented and made copper engravings, surgical instruments, and church bells. His

Paul Revere's skill as a craftsman was much respected. Other craftsmen often copied his designs.

willingness to experiment and take chances served him well both before and after the Revolutionary War.

In Boston during the 1770s, there was tremendous opposition to British taxes and British rule. After the protest known as the Boston Tea Party, Great Britain moved many soldiers into Boston. A clash seemed inevitable. Patriots began collecting weapons and ammunition and storing them in nearby towns, such as Concord. They took part in amateur military drills to get themselves ready to fight the British. They called themselves minutemen because they had to be ready on short notice.

By early 1775 patriots suspected British soldiers were on the verge of leaving Boston for Lexington and Concord to try to seize their weapons. Paul Revere suggested that lanterns be placed in the steeple of Boston's Old North Church to warn people in the countryside. One lantern would mean the British approached on land. Two would indicate they were traveling by water. In addition, he himself would try to ride out of Boston to raise the alarm.

On the evening of April 18, 1775, British soldiers quietly boarded boats.

This engraving depicts Paul Revere's ride through the town of Lexington, during which he warned residents of the British invasion.

Lanterns placed in the steeple of the Old North Church signaled people that the British were leaving Boston for Lexington and Concord.

Minutemen were local citizens who swore to protect their communities from the British. Minutemen received their name because they had to be ready to fight "at a minute's notice."

Two friends rowed Paul Revere a short distance across the water to Charlestown. The patriots there had seen the two lanterns and had a horse ready for Revere. He rode off toward Lexington, stopping at farmhouses and alerting minutemen. At Lexington, Revere warned patriot leaders John Hancock and Samuel Adams that they should go into hiding. Two other men joined Revere at Lexington, and they all rode toward Concord. When the men were halfway to Concord, they were ambushed by British soldiers. They captured Revere, but the other two men escaped and continued on to warn Concord. Near dawn the soldiers freed Revere. He walked toward the center of Lexington early that morning and was rewarded with the sight of the minutemen ready and waiting for the British. It was the beginning of the Revolutionary War.

After the war Paul Revere continued his trade as a craftsman. His silver work is still prized today. Almost one hundred years after Paul Revere's ride, Henry Wadsworth Longfellow memorialized it in a poem, making the remarkable midnight ride one of the best-remembered events of American history.

Paul Revere rode through the night to alert the minutemen that British troops were on the way.

A Delicate Balance

Cape Cod has a problem common to many lovely places. Tourism is the peninsula's main source of income, so the people who live there are dependent on money that tourists spend. On the other hand, too many tourists and too many tourist facilities, such as shops and hotels, destroy the peninsula's natural beauty. Supporting tourism and maintaining nature is a delicate balance.

Cape Cod residents fight hard to preserve the evidence of their past. Nearly every little town has a historical society and a small museum. People work to keep nature unspoiled, too. The 44,000-acre Cape Cod National Seashore is one of the largest coastal nature preserves in the nation. It is home to hundreds of various plant and animal species. In the spring and the fall, the seashore is a resting place for three hundred species of migrating birds. The Wellfleet Bay Wildlife Sanctuary contains salt marsh, freshwater ponds, tidal creeks, sandy beaches, and pine woods.

These people are biking along Cape Cod's Rail Trail.

Grazing Fields Farm is in Buzzard's Bay, just across Cape Cod Canal from the cape itself. The nine-hundred-acre farm has been family-owned since 1907. When Hope Garland Ingersoll's mother bought the land, she cleared only fifty acres for farming and raising horses. The rest was left in its natural state. "We tried to preserve everything," Ms. Ingersoll said. "There was a great variety of wildlife and lots of birds. People like to see wildlife, but you have to have a place that's big enough to support it."

A few years ago, Hope Ingersoll thought Grazing Fields was about to be ruined. The state was planning to modernize the highway into Cape Cod so tourists could get there more easily. The new road would go right through Grazing Fields! Hope Ingersoll and conservation groups fought to save the farm and won. The highway now goes around the farm rather than across it. The battle over the highway had another happy result. Massachusetts passed the Wetlands Protection Act, which is now model legislation for other states that want to pass similar protection laws.

Satisfying both progress and conservation is indeed a delicate balance. But it's well worth the effort on Cape Cod.

Because of erosion and a rising sea level, scientists predict Cape Cod will disappear in less than five thousand years.

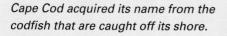

Cape Cod acquired its name from the codfish that are caught off its shore.

27

High Sail to High Technology

They came by sea and lived by the sea. Ever since the first colonists arrived, people in Massachusetts have made their living from the sea. In the first half of the 1800s, things began to change. Cotton mills and shoe factories became more important to the state's economy. Today about 19 percent of the value of goods produced in Massachusetts comes from manufacturing.

The largest area of manufacturing in Massachusetts is the production of scientific equipment and measuring devices. Factories in the Boston area make equipment used for controlling the operations of various automatic machines. They also make equipment used in scientific laboratories.

The production of electrical and communication equipment ranks second in the manufacturing sector of the state's economy. The leading products manufactured in this area are broadcasting equipment, military communications systems, and telephones.

The third largest manufacturing industry in Massachusetts is the production of machinery, especially computers. Companies in Massachusetts began making

The Massachusetts Institute of Technology prepares students for high-tech businesses. The school combines education and research in many different fields, such as medicine, communications, science, and urban studies.

Approximately 23 million tourists visit Massachusetts each year—many of them headed for beaches such as this one on Cape Cod.

computers in the early 1970s. Today, Massachusetts is one of the largest areas of high-tech manufacturing in the country. This distinction, plus the state's many fine universities, attract people interested in high-tech careers. Some of the best engineers and programmers in the world have graduated from Massachusetts universities, especially the Massachusetts Institute of Technology (MIT).

Non-electrical machinery is also an important part of manufacturing in Massachusetts. Although the state's factories do not produce much cloth, they still make the machinery that is used to weave cloth. Massachusetts industries also manufacture printing presses, office machinery, and aircraft engines.

People in Massachusetts also make metal products such as pipes, aluminum windows, metal tanks, valves, knives, and hand tools. In addition, Boston is a major printing and publishing center.

Service industries make up the largest part of Massachusetts economy. Service industries are those in which workers provide a service to other people instead of manufacturing a product. Some services are working in a food store or teaching school. Nearly two-thirds of the state's total economic output is composed of service industries.

The largest section of service industries is in the area of providing community, business, and personal services. Finance, insurance, and real estate services rank second, and wholesale and retail sales rank third.

Wholesale trade is selling goods to businesses, usually in large quantities. Retail trade is selling goods to individual buyers. Other service industries in Massachusetts include working for the government, or working in transportation or communication.

Farming is a small but necessary part of the state's economy. Flowers and ornamental shrubs grown in Massachusetts contribute about one fourth of the state's farm income. The state provides about half the cranberries grown in the United States, too. Milk and other dairy products are the leading source of income from livestock.

Massachusetts is one of the leading states in commercial fishing. New Bedford's catch is more valuable than that of any other United States port. It produces about half the nation's scallops. And Gloucester, the state's second leading port, produces cod, flounder, haddock, ocean perch, and whiting.

The tourist industry provides more income than farming and fishing put together. Every year, tourists spend about six billion dollars visiting historic places such as Boston, Salem, and Plymouth. They relax on the beaches of Cape Cod and other shore resorts. The islands of Nantucket and Martha's Vineyard are also popular tourist sites.

High-tech industries in Massachusetts are helping to build new roads for sending information. They are the pioneers of today's electronic age. The twenty-first century should provide plenty of opportunity for these industries to grow.

Cranberries are the state's second most important farm crop. This tart fruit grows in swampy areas called bogs.

These boats are moored in a Cape Cod harbor. The cape is a major tourist attraction and home to many commercial fishermen.

The Great Experiment

In its time, Lowell, a town in northeastern Massachusetts, was the wonder of the industrialized world. In 1811 Francis Cabot Lowell, a member of one of Boston's richest families, visited Great Britain. He wanted to see the machines of the British Industrial Revolution. He was impressed by the efficiency of making cloth by machine but dismayed at the terrible living conditions of the workers. So when Lowell and his associates planned a mill town on the Merrimack River about 25 miles northwest of Boston, they decided to do things differently.

The town of Lowell was made with concern for the workers' well-being. The workers, mostly New England farm girls, lived in boarding-houses and attended schools and church. The mill also published a magazine called the *Lowell Offering,* which was written by the workers.

At first all went well. The venture was termed a "great experiment." However, good working conditions had

Three of Lowell's factory girls are shown in this nineteenth-century photograph.

This label from a Lowell textile company shows two of the machines that women workers operated for two dollars a week.

been provided to the workers as a gift, not as a right. In the 1840s profits dropped due to increased competition and a depressed economy. The mill owners responded by cutting wages and instituting harsher work rules. The women's wages were about two dollars a week. That was less than one third the average pay for a farm worker. The work was now thirteen-and-a-half hours each day for six days a week. Owners rewarded the supervisors who worked the women the hardest.

In 1844 the women established the Lowell Female Labor Reform Association, and in 1846 they unanimously revolted against the company's newest attempt to increase the workload. But by the end of the 1840s, large numbers of European immigrants had begun arriving in the United States. They were willing to work cheaply and endure harsh conditions. So when the mill workers tried to strike, management simply replaced them. There was an almost endless supply of new labor coming in from overseas. This kept the mills going for many years more. But finally, in the 1930s the last mills closed. Lowell's idea of a Great Experiment was long forgotten. It was replaced by the need to adapt quickly to an ever-changing economy.

Serious About Life
. . . and Art

During colonial times, Massachusetts was the center of literary life. Listing important Massachusetts writers gives an overview of early American literature.

Influential writers in the days of the colonies included Anne Bradstreet, Edward Taylor, and Cotton Mather. Their work reflected the concerns of the Puritan church. Mather, a descendant of several famous Puritan ministers, was a boy genius. By the time he was twelve, he was reading the classics of ancient literature in their original Greek and Latin. In 1675, at the age of twelve, he entered Harvard College. Mather worked as a minister for almost fifty years and wrote more than 450 books. He also founded schools for African Americans and Native Americans.

Phillis Wheatley was the first African American writer published in America. She was born in 1753 in Senegal, Africa, and was brought to Massachusetts as a slave when she was about eight years old. Her owners, John and Susannah Wheatley of Boston, saw that the little girl was very bright. They taught her to read and

This photo depicts the seagoing lifestyle of those who live along the Massachusetts coast.

At Walden Pond, Henry David Thoreau gained great insights by living alone and observing nature.

left. Thoreau lived alone in this one-room cabin from July 4, 1845, to September 6, 1847.

right. Henry David Thoreau was born in Concord in 1817. He studied at Harvard College, where he received his diploma in 1837.

write. She went on to study Latin, astronomy, geography, history, and literature. Phillis began writing poetry at about the age of 13. When she was 20, she traveled to Great Britain, where she read her poems for the public. Phillis was given her freedom when the Wheatleys died.

Concord is a small town less than twenty miles from Boston. During the middle part of the 1800s, it was the home of a group of writers known as the

Transcendentalists. This group of writers rejected the importance of material things. They believed that the mind and the spirit were what counted. Writers who shared this belief included Ralph Waldo Emerson, Henry David Thoreau, Bronson Alcott, and Margaret Fuller. Thoreau is probably the most famous of these writers. He built a small cabin on the shore of Walden Pond, near Concord, where he lived alone for more than two years. While he was there, he thought and wrote about his philosophy of living simply and in harmony with nature. The book Thoreau wrote about his solitary retreat, *Walden, or Life in the Woods*, still inspires thousands of readers.

Emily Dickinson was born in 1830 in Amherst, Massachusetts. She wrote sensitive and original poems about emotions and the imagination. Other important Massachusetts writers of the last century are poet Henry Wadsworth Longfellow, novelist and short-story writer Nathaniel Hawthorne, and novelists Oliver Wendell Holmes and Herman Melville. Melville's most famous novel, *Moby Dick,* is partially based on Melville's own experiences aboard Massachusetts whaling ships.

One of this country's finest and most important African American writers was W. E. B. Du Bois. Born in Great Barrington, Massachusetts, Du Bois was the first African American to receive a Ph.D. from Harvard University. He wrote beautifully and with passion about the need for justice and equality for all people. Du Bois also helped found the National Association for the Advancement of Colored People (NAACP) in 1909. This organization is

Emily Dickinson only had a few of her poems published during her lifetime.

During the middle of the nineteenth century, Henry Wadsworth Longfellow was the most popular poet in the United States.

Dr. W. E. B. Du Bois foresaw that racism would be one of the major problems of the twentieth century.

Winslow Homer's skillful watercolor technique is shown in this 1873 painting, "Boys Wading."

still leading the fight to end discrimination against African Americans.

No discussion of Massachusetts culture can neglect the state's famous painters. John Singleton Copley was America's first notable portrait painter. Samuel F. B. Morse, inventor of the telegraph, was a well-known painter before he ever turned to inventing. John Singer Sargent, another famous portrait painter, lived much of his life in Europe, where he painted the rich and the famous. Winslow Homer, the great painter of the sea, often portrayed the life of New England fishermen. Charles Dana Gibson popularized the "Gibson Girl"—young women dressed in height of turn-of-the-century fashion. Finally, James McNeill Whistler is famous for his "Arrangement in Grey and Black," which is better known as "Whistler's Mother."

Massachusetts is well-represented in music and drama, also. The Boston Symphony Orchestra and the Boston Pops Orchestra are known throughout the world for their high standards. Boston is also the home of choral groups, ballet and opera companies, and dozens of theatrical companies. Many of the state's smaller cities and towns also support music, dance, and theater organizations.

Visitors to Massachusetts can sample the state's artistic tradition, as well as its wealth of history, in its many fine museums. The Boston Museum of Fine Arts and the Boston Institute of Contemporary

Art have world-class collections. The New England Aquarium is home to two thousand species of marine life. Boston's Museum of Science has more than four hundred exhibits and includes a planetarium for guided tours of the stars. Finally, the Boston Children's Museum offers visitors a chance to manipulate objects, perform experiments, and generally see how things work with "hands-on" exhibits.

Much of the culture of Massachusetts arises from its rich history. A great deal of this is preserved in some of Boston's famous buildings, such as the Old State House, built before the Revolutionary War. The Freedom Trail Walking Tour provides a two-and-a-half-mile walk from Boston Commons to Bunker Hill. Along the way are 14 other historic sites, including Paul Revere's home.

From the first days of the Pilgrims and the Puritans, Massachusetts residents have valued the life of the mind and treasured art, literature, and music. It's a tradition nearly four centuries old, and it still flourishes in the Bay State.

The Kennedy children grew up in this house. They included a future President, attorney general, and senator.

Where Art Creates Pride

The residents of the Roxbury section of Boston are mostly African American. It is a lower-income community in which life can be trying and opportunity hard to come by. In 1950 Elma Lewis opened a school there that offered programs to help young men and women find dignity, pride, and self-respect. Today it is more than a school. It is an organization called the National Center for Afro-American Artists (NCAAA).

"People of African descent have been damaged by being without their culture," says Elma Lewis. "So they always feel alien, wherever they are. We investigate and compile the history and culture of people of African descent. Then we teach it and strengthen it."

The Elma Lewis School of Fine Arts is now only one division of the NCAAA. Others include a museum of African culture, an international dance forum, and other arts-related programs.

The Elma Lewis School holds classes in visual arts, music, dance, drama, and costuming. In addition, the school helps students put these skills together for performances. Students perform for schools, camps, churches, and many other audiences. Elma Lewis herself teaches children the fine arts as a way for them to learn about and express their African heritage.

"Arts are not the culture," says Dr. Lewis. "How people live is their culture. It includes how you eat, where you eat, what you eat, how you worship, and what you think. Culture makes you who you are. You express that by your songs, your dances, your poetry, and so on."

Young students learn music at Boston's National Center for Afro-American Artists.

Dr. Elma Lewis opened the first school of the NCAAA in 1950.

The NCAAA welcomes students of all ages.

"It should be normal for people to look at themselves and see beauty," Elma Lewis explains. "It should be normal to them to look at their music, their dance, their visual imagery, the words they speak, and see that they have offered precious things to the world."

The Museum of the NCAAA sponsors a wide variety of programs relating to its exhibits. It once presented a display of objects from the 2,600-year-old pyramid tombs of Nubian kings and queens. The Nubian people had an advanced culture and lived in what is now northeastern Sudan in Africa.

Dr. Lewis believes that learning about African history and culture helps create pride. "We want to give young people standards that will make them overjoyed to be what they are."

She also feels that this pride can combat racism. "My effort has been to impart the dignity of not feeling ugliness toward anybody. If young people are going to succeed, they cannot spend any time considering what anybody thinks about them. I think that would end racism right there, if we all would stop worrying about what other people are thinking and doing."

A Future Rooted in the Past

Massachusetts has so much past that it is sometimes difficult to concentrate on the future. With the momentum of nearly four centuries, great changes and exciting new developments don't come easily. And they shouldn't. Massachusetts is not a place where very many things start from scratch anymore. The new grows out of the old.

Certainly high-tech industries will be a big part of the state's future. But new as these industries might be, they too arise from the past. They're in Massachusetts to take advantage of the universities and the research facilities that have been building for almost four hundred years. They are coming to Massachusetts because their employees want the culture and the quality of life that have been developing since the days of the colonies.

The future of Massachusetts is the payoff on investments made long ago. That's true for the problems as well as for the possibilities. Like other cities around the country, the cities in Massachusetts face

Massachusetts is a leader in environmental protection law. It was one of the first states to safeguard birds, wildlife, tidal marshes, and wetlands.

Boston is building a new sewage treatment plant on Deer Island. Cleaning up sewage helps to reduce water pollution.

their share of problems. Boston in particular suffers from high rates of crime, unemployment, poverty, and urban blight. The need for welfare and social services is large and growing.

Another problem is Boston Harbor, which was one of the most polluted waterways in the United States. For years, untreated sewage from homes and factories ran right into the harbor. Around 1950 the city built two sewage treatment plants, but they weren't large enough for the city's needs. By 1984 harbor fish became poisonous and about 14,000 fishing industry workers had lost their jobs. The water smelled so bad no boaters wanted to be there. State officials created the Massachusetts Water Resources Authority (MWRA) in 1984 to upgrade the old treatment plants and build a new one. Today, the water in Boston Harbor is much improved. Massachusetts and the MWRA continue to look for new ways to upgrade the quality of water throughout the state.

Massachusetts is a treasure store of culture, history, ethnic variety, and tradition. The proud people of Massachusetts are determined that their state's future will be as glorious a contribution as its past has been to the United States.

Important Historical Events

1502 Shipwrecked Portuguese sailor Miguel Cortereal lands on Massachusetts coast.

1602 English explorer Bartholomew Gosnold lands on Cuttyhunk Island. He names it Cape Cod.

1605 Samuel de Champlain from France maps the New England shoreline.

1614 John Smith sails the coast of Massachusetts and writes a book, *A Description of New England*, which later guides the Pilgrims.

1620 The Pilgrims settle at Plymouth.

1621 The Plymouth Pilgrims celebrate their first Thanksgiving.

1630 John Winthrop leads a group of Puritans to Massachusetts and founds Boston.

1641 Massachusetts sets down the first colonial code of laws, called the Body of Liberties.

1692 Twenty people are executed in Salem for practicing witchcraft.

1704 The *Boston News-Letter*, America's first newspaper, begins publication.

1764 British tax laws meet resistance from the colonists.

1770 The Boston Massacre occurs when British soldiers kill five colonists while trying to control an angry mob.

1773 Angry colonists protest a British tea tax by dumping 340 chests of tea into Boston Harbor. This event becomes known as the Boston Tea Party.

1775 The opening shots of the Revolutionary War are exchanged at Lexington and Concord.

1776 American troops under General George Washington drive the British out of Boston.

1786 Shays' Rebellion is staged in front of the courthouse in Springfield by farmers angry over economic conditions.

1788 Massachusetts becomes the sixth state of the Union on February 6.

1814 Francis Cabot Lowell builds one of the first factories in the United States in Waltham.

1831 William Lloyd Garrison of Boston begins publishing his antislavery newspaper, *The Liberator*.

1919 Governor Calvin Coolidge breaks the Boston police strike by sending in the National Guard.

1942 The first United States jet engines are produced at the General Electric plant at Lynn.

1959 The first United States Navy nuclear-powered surface ship is launched at Quincy.

1966 Edward W. Brooke is the first African American to be elected to the United States Senate in the twentieth century.

1974 A federal court orders student busing to achieve immediate racial desegregation in Boston schools.

1988 Governor Michael Dukakis signs a bill that guarantees health insurance to all state residents.

1993 Massachusetts declares the state's school-funding formulas unconstitutional on the grounds that they deny students in poor communities a solid education.

The state flag is white with a royal blue shield in the center. On the shield is a Native American warrior, which is a symbol of Massachusetts. The star represents the state as one of the 13 original colonies. Above the shield is a golden arm holding a saber. On both sides of the shield and across its bottom is a blue banner with the state motto in gold letters.

Massachusetts Almanac

Nickname. The Bay State

Capital. Boston

State Bird. Chickadee

State Flower. Mayflower (trailing arbutus)

State Tree. American elm

State Motto. *Ense Petit Placidam Sub Libertate Quietem* (By the Sword We Seek Peace, but Peace Only Under Liberty)

State Song. "Hail Massachusetts"

State Abbreviations. Mass. (traditional); MA (postal)

Statehood. February 6, 1788, the sixth state

Government. Congress: U.S. senators, 2; U.S. representatives, 10. State Legislature: senators, 40; representatives, 160. Counties: 14

Area. 8,262 sq mi (21,398 sq km), 45th in size among the states

Greatest Distances. north/south, 113 mi (182 km); east/west, 183 mi (295 km). Coastline: 192 mi (309 km)

Elevation. Highest: Mount Greylock, 3,491 ft (1,064 m). Lowest: sea level, along the Atlantic Ocean

Population. 1990 Census: 6,029,051 (5.1% increase over 1980), 13th among the states. Density: 730 persons per sq mi (282 persons per sq km). Distribution: 84% urban, 16% rural. 1980 Census: 5,737,037

Economy. *Agriculture:* greenhouse and nursery products, cranberries, dairy products, hay, apples, beef cattle, eggs, sweet corn. *Fishing:* cod, flounder, scallops, haddock, ocean perch, whiting, lobster. *Manufacturing:* computers and their components, nonelectric machinery, measuring instruments, electrical, scientific, and communications equipment, fabricated metal products, printed materials. *Mining:* crushed stone, sand and gravel, lime

State Seal

State Bird: Chickadee

State Flower: Mayflower

Annual Events

★ Boston Marathon (April)

★ Boston Symphony Pops Concerts in Boston (May/June)

★ Bunker Hill Day in Charlestown (June 17)

★ Blessing of the Fleet in Gloucester (June)

★ Berkshire Music Festival, near Lenox (July/August)

★ Sandcastle Contest, on Nantucket (August)

★ Rowing Regatta in Cambridge (October)

★ Pilgrim Thanksgiving Day in Plymouth (Thanksgiving Day)

★ 12 Days of Christmas in Martha's Vinyard (December)

★ Boston Common Christmas Festival in Boston (November/January)

★ First Night Celebration in Boston (New Year's Eve)

Places to Visit

★ Adams National Historic Site in Quincy

★ Black Heritage Trail in Boston

★ Boston National Historic Park

★ Bunker Hill Monument in Boston

★ Cape Cod National Seashore in southeastern Massachusetts

★ John and Priscilla Alden House in Duxbury

★ Lowell National Historic Park in Lowell

★ Minute Man National Historic Park in Concord

★ Old Sturbridge Village in Sturbridge

★ Plimoth Plantation in Plymouth

★ Ralph Waldo Emerson House in Concord

★ U.S.S. *Constitution*, on the Charles River in Boston

★ Walden Pond, near Concord

★ Whaling Museum in New Bedford

Index